DATE DUE

BOOKINGS & GIGS

Scott Witmer

VISIT US AT

WWW.ABDOPUBLISHING.COM

Published by ABDO Publishing Company, 8000 West 78th Street, Suite 310, Edina, MN 55439.
Copyright ©2010 by Abdo Consulting Group, Inc. International copyrights reserved in all countries.
No part of this book may be reproduced in any form without written permission from the publisher.
ABDO & Daughters™ is a trademark and logo of ABDO Publishing Company.

Printed in the United States.

 PRINTED ON RECYCLED PAPER

Editor & Graphic Design: John Hamilton
Cover Design: John Hamilton
Cover Photo: Getty Images
Interior Photos and Illustrations: AP Images-pg 26; Getty Images-pgs 6, 7, 10, 11, 19, 20, 21, 22, 23, 24, 25, 27, 28; Green Means Go!-pgs 14, 15; iStock Photo-pgs 4, 5, 18; John Hamilton-pgs 8, 9; Jupiter Images-pgs 1, 3; Metric-pg 13; Nuthatch-47-pg 13; Omar Bárcena–pg 25; Red Rocks Amphitheatre-pg 28.

Library of Congress Cataloging-in-Publication Data

Witmer, Scott.
  Bookings & gigs / Scott Witmer.
      p. cm. -- (Rock band)
  Includes index.
  ISBN 978-1-60453-689-8
  1. Rock music--Vocational guidance--Juvenile literature. I. Title. II. Title: Bookings and gigs.
ML3795.W52 2009
781.66023--dc22
                              2009006606

CONTENTS

THE LIVE PERFORMANCE

The lights dim in the arena. The anxious crowd goes silent. Suddenly, the first chords of a song ring out. Spotlights snap on, revealing five rock stars onstage. The crowd goes wild. A roar fills the arena, almost drowning out the music from the band.

There was a time, before CD's, record players, and radio, that a live performance was the *only* way to hear music. It remains the greatest single way to experience any musical art form. But where is the best place to hear live music? Where do bands prefer to play, and how do they arrange these concerts? How do the musicians get paid for these "gigs?"

Scheduling a live performance, or gig, is often called "booking." When rock bands become huge megastars, they have special employees called agents, or booking agents, who arrange these concerts for them. In this book, we will focus mostly on how new and unsigned bands can book gigs themselves.

> Scheduling a live performance for your band is called "booking."

Performing live can be the highlight of any band's career.

First of all, it's important to remember that the music business is just that—a business. Many venues and club owners schedule bands because they truly love music. But most businesses schedule music as a way to make money. This doesn't mean that they don't love live, local music. It just means that they are trying to run a business.

Live bands draw crowds. In addition to buying their tickets, concertgoers also spend money at the venue. Bars and coffee houses often schedule live music to draw in a bigger crowd, which means more sales of drinks and food. And the longer customers stay, the more coffee and cookies and merchandise they will buy.

How are bands paid? Usually, the larger a crowd they can draw, the larger their paycheck will be. Most bars and concert halls pay bands part of "the door," which is money earned from the cost of admission. The more concertgoers who pay to enter, the more money the band will make. Other venues pay bands a guaranteed "flat fee." This is a fixed amount bands are paid to play. Flat fees are usually paid to bands that play several sets over several hours, or for venues that do not have a "cover charge," or admission fee.

A Japanese band that specializes in playing Beatles tunes, performing in a restaurant lounge in Hong Kong, China.

> Bands often are paid part of "the door," which is money earned from the cost of admission. The more people the band attracts to the venue, the more they get paid.

WHERE TO PLAY

For new or unknown bands, there are several opportunities and venues to play music. Even in very small towns, there are many options. Sometimes bands have to be creative in finding locations to play their music.

For almost all bands just starting out, the first place they publicly perform their music is at a private party. These gatherings are very inviting for new bands. Private parties are almost always filled with friends, family, and acquaintances. This is a much more comfortable place to play a first show than in front of a room full of strangers.

In addition to private parties, there are other gatherings where new bands can perform. Many junior high or high schools have talent shows where student musicians can showcase their skills. Talent shows can be a great opportunity for new bands to play for their peers. If your school doesn't host a talent show, don't be afraid to talk to someone in the school administration office about having one.

School talent shows are a great opportunity to play in front of a friendly audience.

Many schools host talent shows where student musicians can showcase their skills.

Like schools, many churches or places of worship also give younger or newer bands an opportunity to showcase their music. In addition to regular worship services, churches host a lot of social events that might feature live music. Perhaps evening socials, or community charity events, or youth ministry events would welcome your music. (But remember, this is probably not the best place to break out your death metal thrash style.)

Many bars and nightclubs feature live music and entertainment as a way to attract customers. Audiences come specifically to hear live music, so bands usually have their full attention. Bars and live music clubs are very helpful to any new band in gaining fans and "buzz." In most bars where alcohol is served, customers must be at least 21 years old. However, some places will allow musicians who are under 21 to perform. Laws vary from state to state. Be sure to find out which laws apply in your location. A nightclub's owner or manager will know if you can legally play.

In addition to bars, there are several other similar businesses that can feature live music. Many coffee houses are popular places today for bands or singer-songwriters to play. Obviously, these venues usually showcase mellower types of music. Most people buying coffee or relaxing with the morning paper will not want to hear your electroclash techno compositions.

Musicians under 21 are allowed to perform at some nightclubs where alcohol is served. Laws are different in each state, so be sure to check with a nightclub's owner or manager before you book a gig at a place that serves alcohol.

As bands become well known, they play larger venues. These places can include amphitheaters, concert halls, and even stadiums. Concert halls and amphitheaters can seat anywhere from 500 to several thousand people. Stadiums can seat up to 100,000 fans, or even more. Large gigs are usually booked by a band's promoter, manager, or record label. However, newer bands sometimes have opportunities to play big gigs. Many cities hold "battle-of-the-bands" contests in larger concert halls. These types of events feature several local bands playing just a few songs each. It can be an excellent way for new bands to gain "big gig" experience. New bands also have a great opportunity to meet and network with other bands at these festivals. Famous bands sometimes recruit local "opening bands" in each city of a national tour. These one-time gigs are often the result of a local contest, or a good band promoter.

Many cities hold "battle-of-the-bands" contests, which give unknown groups a chance to play in large concert halls, or even stadiums.

PRESS PACKETS

Your band has created a demo of songs. You've practiced, rehearsed, and fine-tuned your stage act. You're ready to play in front of an audience. What now? How do you book a gig?

The first important thing to do is prepare a press packet for your band. A press packet is a small package that describes who your band is. It normally includes a picture of your band, plus a demo CD with a few of your best songs. It also should include a "one sheet," a one-page description of your band. The goal of a press packet is to generate excitement. It should represent the best your band has to offer. The press packet should be exciting. It should be interesting enough to catch the eye of a booking agent. Your goal is to convince the agent that *your* band deserves a spot on the agent's performance schedule.

Your band's picture should be tastefully done and highlight the personality of your band. If your band plays serious singer/songwriter compositions, it's probably not a good idea to show band members jumping around on a trampoline in clown suits. If possible, a professional photographer should shoot the photo. However, many upstart bands save money and have a friend shoot a few posed pictures. The most common size for a band portrait is an 8"x10" photo.

Band photos can be shot professionally in a studio, or informally. *Above:* Metric, a Canadian New Wave indie band. *Below:* Nuthatch-47, a Kansas City indie band that blends Russian ska, rock, and blues.

The press packet's demo CD should include approximately 6-10 songs. Edit ruthlessly, including only your band's best material. Remember, more than anything else, it's the demo CD that helps venue owners decide if they want you to play in their businesses. Their time is limited, so hit them with your best shot. If your band composes original songs, the demo should include only your best compositions. If your band plays cover songs (tunes written by other artists), then the demo should include the very best recordings of your band playing these songs.

Finally, the press packet's one-sheet should include a brief summary of what kind of music your band plays. Include a brief history of your band, including any previous gigs you might have played. If your band is searching for its first gig, the one-sheet might include a history of the band members, how the band formed, and how long they have been practicing and writing songs. The most important thing to include on the one-sheet is contact information for your band so the venue owner can schedule a gig. Include an address, phone number, and email address where you can be reached.

A press packet demo CD from indie rock band Green Means Go!

Scott Christensen: Bass
Jake Gronbeck: Percussion
Jason Weidner: Lead Guitar, Vocals
Scott Witmer: Lead Vocals, Guitar

Green Means GO!

Green Means GO! Is a high-energy alternative rock music group from Kansas City, Missouri. The band was formed when mutual friends introduced Scott Christensen and Jason Weidner to Scott Witmer in early 2001. A conversation about music ensued, and a jam session was scheduled. After a few practices with Jason and Scott Witmer on guitar and Scott Christensen on drums, the trio realized they needed a bass player. Scott Christensen volunteered for that spot, but who would play drums? Miraculously, Scott Christensen's roommate, Jake, revealed that he had played drums for over a decade, and eagerly arrived at the next practice. The four had instant chemistry, and wrote several songs that day. After drawing straws to see who would perform lead vocals, a game in which Scott Witmer was the "loser", the lineup was complete. The quartet began to seek gigs, and quickly started playing various bars and clubs in the Kansas City area, and have to date played such venues as The Bottleneck, Davey's Uptown Rambler's Club, America's Pub, The Hurricane, and The Uptown Theater, to name a few.

GMG's musical style is a combination of the four member's individual influences, including late 70's stadium rock, the Motown sound of the 60's and 70's, and mid 90's college radio. Every audience member is looking for something different from a live music experience. Whether you want to dance, groove, jam, or just plain rock, Green Means GO! has something for you. The people you meet at a Green Means GO! show are always a pretty diverse cross section of the Kansas City listening audience.

Due to a continually growing and insistent fan base, Green Means GO! went to Westend Studios to a 5-song demo, and have been working on a full-length independent release during the summer of 2002.

For additional information and/or booking, please contact Scott Witmer

A press packet one sheet from Green Means Go!, the author's former indie rock band based in Kansas City, Missouri.

Once your press packet is prepared, you need to get it into the hands of people who can book gigs for your band. The first step is to find out who is responsible for scheduling at a venue. For most businesses, this information is printed on their website. If not, a quick phone call to the venue will often work. It is very important to find the right person in charge. A personally addressed envelope is much more professional and effective than one that says "Attention: Booking."

Once the correct person is identified, the press packet needs to be delivered. A very common method is simply through the mail. The press packet should be submitted in a professional envelope, clearly addressed, and with a legible return address. Sending press packets through email is becoming more popular. However, email submissions are easy to lose, or be deleted. A physical press packet that a booking agent can touch and feel is almost always best. Remember, the goal of a press packet is to generate excitement about your band.

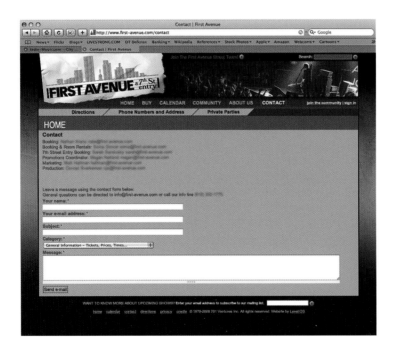

It's very important to find the name of the person who handles bookings for any venue where you want your band to play. The booking agent or promotions coordinator of many venues can be found on their websites, such as this example from First Avenue, the famous nightclub in Minneapolis, Minnesota. If the website doesn't include this information, a polite phone call to the venue will usually work.

According to many booking agents and band managers, it's extremely effective to personally deliver your press packet directly into the hands of the person responsible for booking gigs. The extra time it takes to go to the venue, politely introduce yourself, and personally hand your press packet to the booking agent will make a huge difference. Your band will stand out, and you will have a much better chance of receiving a favorable decision from the booking agent. Booking agents are like normal people: they make better personal connections with someone they have actually met. And they are much more likely to schedule a band they feel they have a personal connection with.

It's common for new bands to mail out press packet after press packet to every venue in town. But then they don't know what to do. They wait for weeks and weeks for a call back. When the call doesn't come, the band assumes that no one wants to book them, and they give up.

Many bands make the crucial mistake of not following up with booking agents. The follow-up call is considered by many to be the most effective way to get your band onto a venue's schedule. Booking agents can receive hundreds of press packets a week. The bands that stand out are the ones that get booked. A quick, courteous call to the booking agent will often do the trick.

Wait about a week after sending your press packet, then call the booking agent. You should identify yourself as a member of the band, then say you called to verify that the booking agent received the press packet. If you handed the packet to the agent personally, ask if they've had a chance to review it. The best approach is to be polite, and keep the conversation short. Booking agents are very busy. They appreciate it if you're considerate of their time.

A single follow-up call is usually best, as opposed to calling over and over again. Remember, the goal is to generate excitement. Nobody wants to work with people who badger them with phone calls.

NETWORKING FOR GIGS

The very best resource new bands can use to get gigs are other bands. Combining resources can be very effective in securing dates to play your music. Upstart groups can be much more successful when working together. Two bands can share their fans, gigs, equipment, and marketing resources. The result is more success, more fans, and more gigs.

"Cross promotion" is when two bands promote their music to each other's fans. The end result is that your band will be able to play for twice as many people. The other band's fans are there already to hear them play, so they will probably listen to your band, too. You'll also have the opportunity to sell twice as many CDs and T-shirts.

MEETING OTHER BANDS

To meet and network with other bands, attend as many local band concerts as you can. Support these groups' music, just like you'd want them to support yours. If you let them know you attend their concerts, there's a good chance they'll come to your gigs. The more people you draw to your shows, the more shows you'll be offered.

> Upstart groups can be much more successful when working together.

If a band plays similar music to yours, there's a good chance they'll be the kind of people you'll become friends with. Remember, even though your goal is to be successful, the reason you're in a band in the first place is to have fun. Having friends in the music business definitely makes it much more fun. The key is to get to know as many local bands as possible. This will give you a lot of exposure in your local scene. You'll also get to see a lot of great live music.

In many cases, when a band is scheduled for a gig, they are allowed to pick their own opening band. If your band picks another band to open your show, chances are they will return the favor when they get their own gig. This means that your band has just received two gigs for the price of one! If your band keeps choosing different opening bands, then soon your band will be asked to play more and more shows. It doesn't take long before a steady stream of concerts will be on your band's calendar.

Even though you want to be successful, remember that the reason you're in a band in the first place is to have fun and make music.

Get to know as many local bands as possible. It will give you a lot of exposure in your local music scene.

AFTER THE GIG

The show is over, but your job is not yet done.

The lights have gone down, the dust has settled, and the crowd has shuffled out the door. What now? A band's job doesn't end after all the equipment has been loaded into the van. There are several things that new bands can do to continue promoting themselves, even after the show. This is the best time to build on your band's "buzz."

A courteous follow-up thank-you call or letter to the booking agent can go a long way to getting future gigs. Most bands do not do this. If you want your band to stand out in a positive way, show appreciation to the person who gave you the opportunity to play. The next time they have cancellations or openings on their calendar, they will remember the band that was kind enough to thank them. This is also an excellent opportunity to get some post-show feedback. Most booking agents attend the shows at their venues. Ask what they thought about your performance. Did they like your sound? Did your band bring in a big-enough crowd? Any helpful suggestions? Booking agents are an invaluable resource when it comes to advice about your new band.

The time after a show is also an excellent opportunity to meet with fans. They're the reason you play in the first place, and their opinion of your show is very important. Be sure to ask what people thought. Remember, you won't please everyone every time, so don't be afraid of negative comments. Constructive criticism can help you grow as a band. This is also a great time to collect email addresses from people who saw your show. Sending a "thank-you" email to fans after a show is a great way to continue promoting your band and keep your fan base growing. This is also a good time to let them know where and when your band will be playing next. The larger your fan base, the more opportunities for gigs you will have in the future.

Throwing yourself into the mosh pit is one way to meet your fans. However you decide to interact with your audience, be sure to ask what they thought of your performance. Constructive criticism can help you grow as a band.

DREAM GIGS

When every band is just starting out, they always have a "dream gig" in mind. It could be the Hollywood Bowl, Madison Square Garden, or the Warped Tour. Many venues are legendary today. These are the shows that young rockers dream to play, or that have altered the course of rock history.

Variety shows have been around since television was invented. These shows feature comedy acts, celebrity hosts, and live music. Today, variety shows remain an important and highly sought-after place for bands to play their music.

Some of the most famous rock-and-roll performances in history have been broadcast on television. On February 9, 1964, The Beatles took America by storm when they performed on *The Ed Sullivan Show*. About 74 million viewers tuned in that night. Many rock historians credit this as the most important rock performance in history. At the very least, it exposed The Beatles to an American audience, and kicked off a worldwide "Beatlemania."

> The Beatles performed on *The Ed Sullivan Show* on February 9, 1964, kicking off their first United States concert tour.

Bands just starting out often have an ultimate "dream gig" in mind. *Above:* The Hollywood Bowl, in Hollywood, California. *Below:* The punk band Less Than Jake playing in Warped Tour '09 in San Francisco.

Woodstock is the most well-known and critically acclaimed rock music festival in history. The concert ran for four days, from August 15th to August 18th, 1969, in Bethel, New York. Thirty-two bands played the festival, all of them major acts at the time. No official count was made of the audience, but some estimate that more than 400,000 people attended. The performances, and the festival itself, became legendary.

Talk shows and sketch comedy shows have propelled many up-and-coming acts into stardom. *Saturday Night Live* has featured musical acts since 1975. Artists from U2 to Britney Spears to The Replacements have played on the show's tiny stage. *Saturday Night Live* is famous for having an instant effect on new artists' stardom. That is why it remains a desirable "dream gig" for many new bands. Late-night talk shows, such as *The Tonight Show*, or *Late Show with David Letterman*, are also known for being prestigious gigs.

Musical guest Spoon performing on *Saturday Night Live* on October 6, 2007.

> Guitar-legend Jimi Hendrix playing live at Woodstock.

An estimated 400,000 people attended the 1969 Woodstock music festival.

Since Woodstock, many other promoters have attempted to duplicate its success. There are still several yearly music festivals around the world that bands aspire to be invited to. Coachella takes place in Indio, California. Bonnaroo Music and Arts Festival is in Tennessee. South By Southwest and the Austin City Limits Music Festival are both held in Austin, Texas. England hosts the Glastonbury Festival of Contemporary Performing Arts. There are also several traveling festivals. These are held at multiple locations over several dates. Famous examples include the Warped Tour, Ozzfest, and Lollapalooza.

Another highly desired gig for bands is to play at a major stadium or amphitheater. Stadiums can seat 100,000 people or more. They are considered possible venues only for the very top tier of musical acts. The first rock band to ever play a true stadium was The Beatles, at New York City's Shea Stadium, on August 15, 1965. More than 50,000 people saw the show. Other famous stadiums and amphitheaters include Madison Square Garden in New York City, Wembley Stadium in London, England, Red Rocks Amphitheatre in Denver, Colorado, and The Hollywood Bowl in Hollywood, California.

Red Rocks Amphitheatre in Denver, Colorado.

Perry Farrell and guest guitarist Slash perform at the 2008 Lollapolooza music festival in Chicago, Illinois.

GLOSSARY

BOOKING AGENT
An employee of a band or venue who arranges concert dates. Usually, only established bands can afford booking agents. Bands that are just starting out must learn how to arrange gigs on their own.

BUZZ
Word-of-mouth discussions about your band. If your performances generate a lot of positive buzz, your audiences will almost certainly grow.

CONSTRUCTIVE CRITICISM
A kind of advice that points out how artists can improve. Instead of merely putting down a group's performance, constructive criticism can be used to make future performances even stronger.

COVER CHARGE
An admission fee. The amount of money a person pays to see a live band play at a venue such as a concert hall, bar, or lounge.

CROSS PROMOTION
When two or more bands team up and work together to promote each other's music and concerts. Cross promotion can greatly increase the number of fans who show up to hear a band play.

DEMO CD
A CD of about 6-10 of a band's best songs. Demo CDs are given to potential venues or booking agents in the hope of being asked to play a live gig.

Door

Bands are often paid part of "the door," which is the money the venue makes by charging admission. If a band is popular, more people pay admission. The larger door means a bigger paycheck for the band.

Flat Fee

Sometimes bands are paid a certain amount of money, a "flat fee," for playing a gig, no matter how big an audience shows up to hear them play.

Gig

A job as a musician, often a live performance.

One Sheet

A single sheet of paper that describes your band, including the kind of music you play, a brief history of the band and its members, and any previous gigs that you've played.

Press Packet

A package of materials used to market a band. Press packets usually include a demo CD, a one sheet describing the band, and a photo of the band members.

Record Label

A company that manages, produces, markets, and distributes music and music videos by various bands. The "label" in the name refers to the days when music was mainly recorded on vinyl disks. The company's logo, plus song information, was printed on a circular sticker placed in the center of the record.

Venue

The place where a concert is performed.

INDEX